HEALING
RELATIONSHIPS
THROUGH FORGIVENESS

DISPLAYING GOD'S GRACE
TO OTHERS

A GROUP STUDY
PART 3

DONALD E. JONES, PHD

J & A BOOK PUBLISHERS
www.jabookpublishers.com

ISBN-13: 978-0692702543
ISBN-10: 0692702547

DEDICATION

I dedicate this book to my Savior and Lord Jesus Christ. He has been with me every step of my journey upon the earth, and I so look forward to being in His presence forever and ever.

CONTENTS

ACKNOWLEDGMENTS

I want to thank my wonderful and gracious wife Carol who has supported me in this ministry with sacrifice, enthusiasm, encouragement, and accountability. Most of all, she has been a constant blessing because of her willingness to listen. I was always sharing with her the truths God had been teaching me as I studied His word and wrote this book. It consumed many hours. Thank you, Carol and I deeply love you.

I want to thank my son Gregory R. Jones for volunteering to be the primary editor of this important book. Without his time and effort in painstakingly and meticulously going over every word and every sentence checking and rechecking the sentence structure and grammar, I would not have been able to complete it. Thank you for your ministry to me.

I want to thank my other children, Krista, Matt, and Kara for their love for Christ and His Word and their willingness to live for Him. I love you all.

Introduction

This series of three books (Part 1,2,3) grew out of a desire to put the material in my main book on healing relationship through forgiveness into a format for small group study. As a result, the introductions are the same in all three books. This is primarily due to the essential nature of the content in our understanding of the truths found in each one. It also allows the books to be read and studied one after the other or to be studied independent of the other two. This provides more flexibility to the various individuals, groups, churches, and organizations who wish to use it.

After Moses had received the Ten Commandments, the prophet and leader requested that God show him His glory. The Almighty explained to Moses that no human could see Him and live. Nevertheless, God would grant his request by allowing His servant Moses to experience the passing of His "goodness" by him and the actual viewing of the "backside of His glory." On the next morning, he stood upon a rock and called upon the name of the Lord. The Lord God descended in the form of a cloud, shielded Moses in the cleft of the rock, and covered him with His divine hand. As God displayed His divine glory visibly, He declared the many attributes of His supernatural, divine character.

In Exodus 34:6-7, Moses described this amazing moment and the words that he heard the Lord declare about Himself. The prophet recorded, "Yahweh [I AM THAT I AM] passed by before him...he proclaimed, 'Yahweh! Yahweh, a merciful and gracious God, slow to anger...abundant in His loving kindness and truth, keeping loving kindness for thousands, forgiving iniquity and disobedience and sin.'" A book that is written on healing relationships through forgiveness by its nature must begin with the proclamation that the God of the universe is not only the merciful, gracious, patient, loving, kind, truth-filled, just, and righteous Lord but an Almighty deity who "forgives iniquity, transgressions, and sin." This Lord God announced that He is a "forgiving" God.

This by no means negates the fact that He is also a just and righteous one; therefore, this forgiveness comes with a price that had to be paid. So, He sent His Son to die to pay the penalty for our sins in order to pour out His forgiveness upon all mankind. Through faith in Jesus Christ, men and women experience the full extent of His forgiveness that was proclaimed to Moses many years ago on that mountain top. Once this has occurred in our lives, we are to live for Him. We are to act like Him, and we are to obey Him. One of the critical ways in which God desires His forgiven people to live for, act like, and obey Him is *to forgive others as we are forgiven*. This is the key point of these books. As the Lord God has forgiven us and healed our relationship with Him, He requires us to forgive and heal our relationships with others. This is found in several passages in the Scriptures. Two of them are mentioned by our Lord and one from the apostle Paul. All three clearly explain the important truth that relationships are to be "reconciled" and "restored" to "gain back" one's brother, sister, or neighbor. This is done primarily through forgiveness.

In Matthew 5, the Lord Jesus discusses the heart attitudes people in His kingdom should possess. After speaking of anger, the Lord presents a general principle of living in His kingdom on earth. In verses 23-24, He explains, "If therefore you are offering your gift at the altar, and there remember that your brother has anything against you, leave your gift there before the altar, and go your way. First be reconciled to your brother, and then come and offer your gift." The Greek word translated "reconciled" means "to make changes." It originates from a Greek root word that was a banking term meaning "to render accounts the same." There would be a discrepancy between two bank ledgers, and all the mistakes would have to be found and corrected in order for them to agree. We express this between people as "being on the same page." The Lord Jesus indicates that the Father desires His people to come to Him fully reconciled with each other. If we, as Christians, know that someone harbors something against us, we are to take the initiative and go to them and reconcile with them. We should not wait for them to come to us. We take our responsibility and go to them. We must once again "settle accounts." They have the same responsibility.

In Matthew 18, Jesus discusses those who are sinning in the church and what all believers should do. In verse 15, the Lord commands, "If your brother sins against you, go, show him his fault between you and him alone. If he listens to you, you have gained back your brother." The Greek word translated "gain" refers "to obtaining or securing something." When a relationship is restored, we gain back everything that the other parties contributed. In this particular case, we have something against our brother, rather than the reverse. If this does happen, we are to take the initiative and confront our brother or sister to gain him or her back and restore the relationship. So, whether someone has something against us, or we have something against someone else, the procedure is essentially the same. Christians must take the initiative and reconcile with them.

The third passage involves the restoration of a sinning brother in the church. In Galatians 6, Paul opens the chapter with an explanation of how to help a sinning saint. In verse one, Paul asserts, "Brothers, even if a man is caught in some fault, you who are spiritual must restore such a one." The Greek word translated "restore" means "to render fit, sound, or complete; to mend or repair what has been broken." The word is used of a physically broken fishing net. In Mark 1:19

3

and Matthew 4:21, when Jesus called James and John into ministry with Him, they were in the process of "mending" their fishing nets. They were mending the holes in their net so the fish would not fall through. This restoration could easily involve a conflict between two people. The holes in their relationship need to be mended. This process involves healing relationships through forgiveness. These passages will be referred to as you read.

These books are my original works on reconciliation and forgiveness. It is not based on other books that I have read and simply collated. To produce this work, I carefully read through the entire New Testament verse by verse. Then, I meticulously perused the Old Testament paying particular attention to the Psalms and Proverbs. As I read, categories were built from the individual passages, rather than a set of preconceived notions. These numerous categories became the individual biblical principles found in every chapter. Each passage was studied in its historical, grammatical, and scriptural contexts. After this, I compared my interpretations with those of past and present scholars. After this study, I have attempted to follow these biblical principles in my own personal life and also utilize them in my pastoral counseling practice. I have seen the Holy Spirit use them to transform relationships of all kinds.

One last thought. At the end of each chapter, I discuss a counseling experience. Due to confidentiality, none of these are based on one particular counseling situation. Instead, I have mixed together common elements I have seen, details from books and films, bits from my own life and the lives of people I have known, and thoughts from my imagination to create a situation where the biblical principles discussed in the chapters can fully be applied. These are composites of real-life situations. Read, learn, and apply. I commend you to the Lord and His Word (Acts 20:32).

Chapter 1

Forgive as Forgiven

In part two of this three-part series of books, we discussed the gentle confrontation of sin. We must confront those who have sinned against us. This would occur after we had asked them for forgiveness even if they started the conflict. This was the last step in that process. We also viewed the gentle confrontation of sin as the initial step to take when others have transgressed us. After this, the action that should be taken by Christians should be to forgive as they are forgiven. This will not be easy and is a divine act. It is important to note that this forgiveness is not dependent on others asking for our forgiveness first. It is not a result of their acceptance of the consequences either. True believers simply forgive as God has forgiven them when the Holy Spirit convicts them. This will not be easy because it requires a supernatural, divine act.

A Typical Scenario

Have you ever had or heard a conversation with a spouse, parent, or friend about a co-worker that went something like this? You say, "I cannot believe he stole my idea at work. I came up with the basic concept of the new company logo and showed it to him. He went to our boss and said it was his. I am so angry. If he ever comes to me and begs for my forgiveness, I'm not forgiving him. He can crawl on his hands and knees, but it will not do any good." This simple scenario illustrates the fact that sometimes, we do not want to forgive others for what they have done to us. Sometimes the transgression is so hurtful that it becomes difficult to overcome. Other times, we will not forgive out of pure pride or stubbornness. This does not sit well with our Lord. He forgives us all that we do each and every day, and He requires His children to act like Him and do the same.

A Scriptural Principle

The first principle in the forgiveness process is "we must forgive others as we have been forgiven." This principle encompasses has several important aspects. First, we must forgive all transgressions, nothing can be held back. Second, we must forgive all people, no one can be excluded. Third, we must forgive all the sins of all the people because we have been forgiven all our sins. Why are we to do this? The primary reason is that God expects His children to behave like Him. Since He has forgiven all the transgressions of believers, so they are to do the same.

A Biblical Explanation

Our God is a God that forgives. It is a part of His divine nature. In Micah 7:18-19 the prophet makes this declaration, "Who is a God like you, who pardons iniquity, and passes over the disobedience of the remnant of his heritage?" God, our Father, pardons all our transgressions and passes over all our disobedience. Then Micah adds, "He doesn't retain his anger forever, because he delights in loving kindness." When His anger is kindled toward our sin, it subsides in the light of his love and kindness. The prophet asserts, "He will again have compassion on us. He will tread our iniquities under foot; and you will cast all their sins into the depths of the sea." In God's compassion all our sins are cast away and tread under his foot. We studied numerous passages in the Scripture that teach the full and total forgiveness of all sins.

6

This occurred at the cross and was appropriated to us when we received Christ as Savior and Lord. We were declared righteous (justified) before God for all eternity (Romans 3:24, 28; 4:5).

When we sin on earth as we await our eternal dwelling place, we maintain a relationship with the Lord. At times, our flesh gets control, and we sin (James 1:14). That sin must be dealt with through confession (1 John 1:9). When we confess our sins, God is faithful to forgive us all our sins. This is a relational forgiveness. In our relationship with Him, His love, grace, and compassion proceed from Him and cover over all our sins that are against Him. He desires that same compassion, love, and grace to cover over the sins of others against us in forgiveness. He wants His people to tread the transgressions of others under their feet and cast them in their minds as far away as the depths of the sea!

Next, God does not make any distinctions in forgiveness when it comes to His people. All are forgiven. One of the issues, Paul encountered in the churches was a distinction the Christians were making among themselves. Since the Jews were originally God's people, they thought they were above the Gentiles. Paul spent so much time explaining to both groups, God does not make distinctions among people when it comes to His forgiveness and blessings. In Ephesians 3:6, Paul discloses, "That the Gentiles are fellow heirs, and fellow members of the body, and fellow partakers of his promise in Christ Jesus through the Good News." Then in Galatians 3:28, the apostle speaks against other distinctions, "There is neither Jew nor Greek, there is neither slave nor free man, there is neither male nor female; for you are all one in Christ Jesus." All people are forgiven no matter what differences they may have. Though this may seem obvious, it is not always practiced. Instead, we tend to want to forgive some and not others who have wronged us.

In Corinth, the church made distinctions based on which leader one followed or who had what gifts of the Spirit. In 1 Corinthians 1:13, Paul asks the powerful question, "Is Christ divided?" The answer to this rhetorical question was no. As a result, we also may not divide Him by making distinctions. In 1 Corinthians 12:13, Paul says, "For in one Spirit we were all baptized into one body, whether Jews or Greeks, whether bond or free; and were all given to drink into one Spirit." We cannot make distinctions in our forgiveness of others. Why? The Lord makes no distinctions in His forgiveness of us. This means we can make no distinctions in our forgiveness of other believers. We cannot say, "I do not like him, and I will not forgive him." The flesh can create in our minds some of the most ridiculous excuses for why we shouldn't forgive. We cannot succumb to its seemingly rational reasons which are utterly sinful. All believers are to be forgiven all sins without distinctions.

If all believers should be forgiven their sins without any distinctions made, what about unbelievers? Should we make any distinctions among those who do not know Jesus Christ concerning forgiveness? The answer is found in the answer to another question, "Does God call all people to salvation and forgiveness?" In 1 Timothy 2:3, Paul entreated Timothy, his son in the faith, to pray for the salvation of all people, He wrote, "For this is good and acceptable in the sight of God our Savior." Then in verse four, Paul provided the important reason, "Who desires all people to be saved and come to full knowledge of the truth." So, we must forgive all people.

There were some people mocking believers because they were claiming that Christ was coming back, and He had not yet come. In 2 Peter 3:9, Peter proclaimed, "The Lord is not slow concerning his promise, as some count slowness; but is patient with us, not wishing that any should perish, but that all should come to repentance." Our God desires all people to find forgiveness in His only Son. He does not make any distinctions. This means that the Father desires His children in the same way to also forgive people their transgressions. We cannot say, "He's an unbeliever or (insert some criticism here), and I will not forgive him."

The Lord taught the following principle throughout His ministry. If God forgives the sins of all of us against Him, then we are to forgive the sins against us. In Matthew 6:12, during the Sermon on the Mount, Jesus explained that the prayers of God's kingdom people should conclude with these words, "Forgive us our debts, as we also forgive our debtors." In Mark 11:25, on His way to Jerusalem, Jesus told His disciples, "Whenever you stand praying, forgive, if you have anything against anyone." In Luke 11:4, when He was asked how to pray, Jesus Christ delivered the Lord's Prayer for a second time which included the forgiveness of others. He said, "Forgive us our sins, for we ourselves also forgive everyone who is indebted to us." Notice, the Lord makes no distinction between believers and unbelievers in His words. The Lord Jesus uses the inclusive terms "debtors," "anyone," and "everyone." Forgiveness is extended to all.

In Ephesians 4:31-32, concerning believers, Paul exhorted, "Let all bitterness, wrath, anger, outcry, and slander, be put away from you, with all malice." Here is a list of terrible sins and transgressions believers may commit toward us and us toward them. They may become angry, bitter, hot-tempered and then yell, scream, lie, plot, and gossip about us. We may do the same to them. He commands us to stop this sin and behave in a wholly different way. Paul continues, "And be kind to one another, tenderhearted, forgiving each other, just as God also in Christ forgave you." When these harsh and cold transgressions occur against us, we should not respond in the same way. Instead, we must be kind, compassionate, tender, and then forgive them fully as God did us.

This was such an issue in the churches that Paul had to speak of it again in his letter to the church in Colossae. This inspired writer in Colossians 3:12-13 explained what their "wholly different" behavior should be, "Put on therefore, as God's chosen ones, holy and beloved, a heart of compassion, kindness, lowliness, humility, and perseverance." These are the divine qualities of our Father. When transgressed, he continues with these words, "Bearing with one another, and forgiving each other, if any man has a complaint against any; even as Christ forgave you, so you also do." As our God is pouring out His forgiveness upon us every day of our lives, we, as His people, are to be pouring out our forgiveness on others every day.

Jesus also delineated the consequences if God's kingdom people did not forgive. In these same passages, Jesus warns His followers. In Matthew 6:14-15, He beseeches, "For if you forgive men their trespasses, your heavenly Father will also forgive you. But if you don't forgive men their trespasses, neither will your Father forgive your trespasses." In Mark 11:25, He declares, "Whenever you stand praying, forgive, if you have anything against anyone; so that your Father, who is in heaven, may also forgive you your transgressions." The Lord is not talking about eternal forgiveness, but here again relational forgiveness on this earth. This is the kingdom life of believers on this earth with their God. God forgives them, and they forgive others. If we want things to be right with God in our lives, we need to be behaving towards others as He behaves towards us. We need to act just like Him. If not, we should expect the process of discipline and training to begin in order that we become more like His Son in this area.

Now, how does this work in real life? When we become filled with anger and bitterness and unwilling to forgive, we must consider the amount and extent of the transgressions we have committed against God. He has made absolutely no distinctions in forgiving us. Then we will discover that the sins against us will look so much smaller in comparison to our large number of sins against God. After this, our hearts will be opened to His Spirit through this biblical truth. Then God's mercy, grace, and love that was shown and is shown every day to us in forgiveness, will pour forth into our own love, grace, and mercy in forgiveness toward others. People struggle with forgiveness when they forget how much they have been forgiven. Sometimes, they may be too proud to realize what horrible sinners they are!

When believers are continually coming before the throne of God begging God for forgiveness, they will understand be able to forgive in a greater way whether the transgressors are believers or not. One of the primary ways Christians can have growing relationships with spouses, parents, children, friends, church members, co-workers, fellow students, and acquaintances is through this constant confession process. We admit our sins, accept His forgiveness, and then provide the same toward all others. The Lord does not desire that we make any distinctions between people when it comes to the forgiveness toward others. Forgiveness for all believers and unbelievers should pour from our hearts.

Also, the forgiveness of others does not necessarily occur after we gently confront them with their sin, and they ask for forgiveness. It could happen as the sin is occurring or even immediately afterward. Every sin someone commits against us cannot possibly be confronted. There are simply too many annoyances and little sins. God certainly does not confront us on every sin we commit, nor does He discipline us. We cannot wait for those who have sinned against us to ask for forgiveness because often they do not or will not. Forgiving others is not dependent on their response but only on God's forgiveness of us. If our forgiveness was solely dependent on waiting for them to ask, then we would be full of bitterness.

An Ancient Portrait

This principle is beautifully illustrated in the "Parable of the Unforgiving Debtor" in Matthew 18:23-35. Peter had just inquired of the Lord as to whether seven times is enough to forgive someone who had sinned against us. To him that seemed pretty reasonable. To Jesus, it was absurd. Instead, Jesus told him it was more like "seventy times seven." This meant as many times as needed. Then to help His disciples understand the absolute importance of forgiving others as many times as they sin against them, He tells this powerful story that speaks directly to the issue.

Jesus begins the story by describing a king who desired to settle accounts with his servants. These were not his slaves in chains but probably provincial governors. They were to pay the king his legal share of their tax revenue in order to support the kingdom. This king discovered that one of his "servants" owed him ten thousand talents. To owe him this much, the governor would have to have kept back the owed tax revenues for many years. It became an impossible sum to pay back. In modern terms, we would owe back taxes, so large that we could not pay them back no matter how long we worked. This man was in a difficult predicament.

The tax revenue of Judea and Samaria together was only two to three hundred talents, so one can imagine the great sum ten thousand would be. The point is simple: it was an impossible sum to ever pay back. When the king discovered the discrepancy, he would have known that the servant had been cheating the king for a very long time. This would have made him extremely angry. Since he obviously couldn't pay, the king ordered him to be sold into slavery with his whole family. Then whatever he owned would be sold, so some payment could be made. This would come nowhere near the amount owed, but the king would take everything.

To take all that the man owned and to sell his family into slavery would never earn the king enough to compensate for all the man had stolen. It would cost the servant everything that he had and beyond. This was a common practice among the nations in the ancient world. Everyone who heard Jesus would understand what was described. So, this official fell to the ground in submission and worship and began to beg for mercy from the king. He cried, "Please, please, be patient and I will repay you!" This would have been impossible, and they both knew it but crying out for the king's patience and mercy was his only hope.

He did not deny his sin or question the king's judgment. He pleaded for mercy! Suddenly, this king felt compassion for the man and released him from the debt. He could have lambasted him for such a ridiculous request, but he did not. He bestowed complete forgiveness on the man and wiped away his debts. The official walked away a free man and unencumbered from any transgressions. He had pleaded for mercy and received it. Does this not sound like believers who plead for mercy, receive Christ as Savior and Lord, and are released from all the debts of their sin? Yes, it does, and this is the first point Christ is making to Peter.

Then, something utterly hypocritical happened. The man immediately proceeded to behave in a way that was almost exactly opposite of the forgiveness the king had shown him. Obviously, while he was trembling before the patient king, he must have remembered that someone else should actually be trembling before him. Once released, the official decided to search for the man who had owed him some money, and he would not receive the same kind of mercy from him. He did not care that in comparison to the debt that was just forgiven; it was a small amount of only one hundred denarii. When he found him, he grabbed him by the throat since the debtor was on the same level as him (a fellow-servant).

While the first servant's hands were wrapped around his throat choking him, the official demanded payment of what he was owed. So, this fellow-servant did exactly what the official had just done to the gracious king. He begged for mercy from him. He fell down to the ground in submission and cried, "Please, please be patient, and I will repay you." Since this amount was so much smaller, this man's payback was actually possible.

Though the official had been shown compassion when he uttered those words, he responded in a completely opposite manner. There was no compassion, no mercy, and absolutely no love. He threw the fellow-servant into prison until this man paid back every denarius he owed. Unfortunately for the official, a group of his own people (fellow-servants to the king) happened to be strolling by. The Lord Jesus described his actions as grieving them terribly, so they all left to report it to the king in detail. They knew that this was unacceptable behavior for someone who had just received so much mercy! When the king discovered what the grievous act his official had committed, the official was summoned.

As this servant stood before him a second time, the king rebuked him and said, "You wicked servant! I forgave all the debt you had because you pleaded with me. Couldn't you have had mercy on your fellow-servant in the same way that I had mercy on you?" Notice this sovereign rebuked the man for not following his example. Then his majesty became angry and commanded that the servant be handed over to the torturers until all of the ten thousand talents had been repaid. Of course, this was impossible, so he would spend his life in prison. At this point the Lord Jesus ends the story and issues a warning, "So will the heavenly Father do to you, if you don't forgive your brother from the heart!" What an indictment! These were stern words from the Master! What could Jesus have meant?

Here Jesus (the master) was talking to Peter and His other disciples! He is not speaking to unbelievers because God is not their heavenly Father! He may be their creator, but He is not their Father. Rather than interpreting every detail of the parable, which is not necessary, let's get to Jesus' second point. The debt of our sin against God is so great that we could not pay it back in an eternity of punishment or a lifetime of good deeds (the torture until paid back). The sins people commit against us, no matter what they consist of, are very small in comparison to our sins against God (ten thousand talents vs. one hundred). As He demonstrated full and complete forgiveness of our sins, we are to do the same to others (the king felt compassion and released him). If not, we will experience the discipline and training of the Lord, and it will not be pleasant (threw him into prison)!

A Modern Anecdote

Due to a large immigration movement, the population of the western world now represents many different cultures and values. As people of different cultures meet, fall in love, marry, and raise children in their new country, often there is a clash of cultural values between the children and parents within the family. Though she did not know it at the time, this was the issue that one such young lady was facing when she came in for counseling.

She explained that she had problems in her relationships with men. As soon as she came near to "falling in love," the young lady would inevitably push the men away. She could accomplish this feat by providing numerous "mixed signals." This would utterly confuse the men so they would give up and end the relationship. Though she thought about it often, the young lady could not figure out the real reason for this endless cycle of confusing suitors.

15

After a short time, we discovered that she had unresolved issues with her father. Though this might not always be the case, it was with her. She felt that her father had treated her mother in a demanding and demeaning way, and she did not like it. When I asked for examples, she told me that her father bossed her mother around and expected her mother to obey every command of his. She described her mother as acting like "like a little puppy dog" following him all around the house. He spoke and she listened. Whatever her father wanted, her mother did. This angered her greatly.

When I probed further, she gave more specific details. He would ask her to get him a drink of water, and she would run to get it. Though he could have gotten up and served himself. Also, he wanted dinner on the table as soon as he got home and refused to ever help her in the kitchen. The daughter was appalled. Sometimes, his tone of voice became harsh and unkind. When she left for college, she was so glad to get out of the house and be rid of him once and for all.

Then she ran out of money and had to move home. Now, she was back in this toxic environment. The father's behavior did appear a bit out of sync with western cultural norms, but it was not abusive. I asked her if he had ever mistreated her, and she said, "Never! In fact, he always treated me better than my mom. It made me suspicious that it was all an act. I don't trust men." Why should she? She thought that the most important man in her life had failed her, why would she trust another man? After discovering that her mother and father were immigrants from different cultures, things began to clear up. We took some time to study how the roles of men and women differed in the cultures of her parents and then the western culture she had embraced.

It dawned on her that her father was simply following the cultural values of the country he came from. Though the mother's values were less restrictive than her husband's, she loved him and enjoyed caring for him. She did not mind acting in accordance with his views. It was the daughter that did not like it. She was viewing the situation from a third western cultural perspective. When she was asked if she had ever shared her feelings with her father, she responded, "No! He is evil and wouldn't understand." I explained to her from the Scriptures that God desired her to gently confront him. He certainly deserved the chance to explain his actions at the very least.

Gentle confrontation is not simply to blast a person for his sin, but to see the situation from both sides. She also needed to consider that she may have been wrong in her view of his behavior over these years which led to her intense bitterness toward him. She might well have been angry because she misunderstood her parents' views of their different cultural roles. She would need to repent of this anger and ask for her father's forgiveness. Whatever she decided to do, God would want her to forgive her father just as He had forgiven her for whatever wrongs she had committed in her life.

When she heard this, she stood up and marched out of my office. I heard her mumbling, "I'll never forgive him!" A month later, she gave me a call to let me know that the Holy Spirit had deeply convicted her for the bitterness. The Holy Spirit always convicts of sin and encourages us to act on it.

So, she decided to go to her father and gently confront the man. After an extremely long conversation, she finally began to understand him better. He explained to her how much he loved her and how sorry he was. She told him how sorry she was for harboring such bitterness for so long. This restored the relationship, and they began the process of building it to a new level. This came about because the young woman was willing to gently confront her father. We must do the same.

A Personal Response

Dear Heavenly Father,

After studying the principles in this chapter, I realize that I have made distinctions in my forgiveness. I have forgiven others but not (add name) for (add sin). It has been really difficult because of (describe issue). Help me remember how much you have forgiven me on a daily basis. I know I have done much worse to You when I (describe sins). I know the amount my transgressions against you far outweigh (add names)'s sin against me. I am sorry for my hardened heart. Please help me to forgive (add name). I want to honor You in my relationship with (add name) and follow Your Word. I pray this in the name of Jesus. Amen.

Chapter 2

Forgive the Forgiven

From practical experience, we know that when Christians have transgressed us, it is not always easy to forgive them. Believers can commit some horrible sins against us that can do great damage to our lives and the lives of those we love. Many people can share stories of believers in a local church who have hurt them. The church has problems because it is made up of people who have problems. The real question is, "How do we handle these problems when they arise?" We are to forgive. Sometimes, this is difficult. When this occurs, one way of resolving this dilemma is to consider all the sins that we have committed against God. God has forgiven so much more. We put away any distinctions in who they are or what they have done to us and forgive. In this chapter, we will learn that not only should we forgive believers because we are forgiven, but also because they are already forgiven by the Lord God.

A Typical Scenario

Have you ever had or heard a conversation with a spouse, parent, or friend about another friend that went something like this? You say or hear, "Do you see my magazine? I just loaned it to my friend. His two-year-old son got ahold of it, and now it is destroyed. I was going to pass the magazine to my brother. He loves these things. Every time I have loaned this guy something, it happens again. I am done. I have had enough with him. I am so angry! (Person comments.) What? I don't care if he is a Christian. If he ever comes to me and asks for forgiveness, I'm not forgiving him. And don't quote me any Bible passages. I will never ever forgive him. Do you really understand? Never!"

A Scriptural Principle

We must once again begin thinking differently about the person and the transgression to overcome this problem. This brings us to principle two which is "we must know that believers who transgress us are already forgiven for their sins." This is an obvious truth, but it is not often considered in this type of circumstance. Whether Christians who have transgressed us have asked for our forgiveness or not, our holy God and Father has already forgiven them eternally. Whether those who sin against us have asked Him for forgiveness or not, the Lord will handle that relationally. Whether the saints who have sinned against us have asked for forgiveness or not, God will also handle that issue with them as He handles the issue with us.

That is the direct work of His Spirit. We can confront, but He has to work in their hearts. If we have difficulty forgiving another believer, we must consider that those sins against us were nailed to the cross when they received Jesus as Savior and Lord. We may claim all the forgiveness that God gives to us, but we don't always want to think that the Lord has already forgiven the sins they have committed against us through Christ's death on the cross (Colossians 2:13-14).

A Biblical Explanation

Let us study God's forgiveness, not in the light of our own sins, but in the light of deeds against us by other Christians. In the introduction of this book, I mentioned Exodus 34:6-7. In this passage, Moses asked God if he could see His glory.

God could only allow him to see the backside, as it were, so He would not be consumed. As God physically manifested Himself to Moses, you may remember that He also verbally declared his glory with these words, "Yahweh passed by before him, and proclaimed, "Yahweh! Yahweh, a merciful and gracious God, slow to anger, and abundant in loving kindness and truth, keeping loving kindness for thousands."

Now, let's read the last part of God's revelation about His character with the wicked deeds of believers against us in our minds. The Lord is "forgiving iniquity and disobedience and sin" of other saints against us. God's glory is manifested when He forgives the sins of others against us. It is a part of God's nature to forgive the sin of other believers against us. His forgiveness extends not only to our sins against others but to others' sins against us. One of the primary reasons we are to forgive is that they are already forgiven by our God. They transgressed against Him first. Yet, God had enough grace, mercy, and love to forgive them and so should we.

In Luke 17:3-4, Jesus teaches, "Be careful. If your brother sins against you, rebuke him. If he repents, forgive him." He commands forgiveness of others again. Then Jesus exhorts, "If he sins against you seven times in the day, and seven times returns, saying, 'I repent,' you shall forgive him." Why should we? One reason is that God, our Father, has already forgiven them. In Matthew 26:28, at the last supper, Jesus proclaimed, "For this is My blood of the covenant, which is poured out for many for forgiveness of sins." The blood of Christ was not simply poured out for us and the sins we commit against others but also poured out for others and the sins they commit against us. What an amazing change in perspective. So, when I consider the sins of a spouse, parent, child, friend, fellow student, co-worker, or neighbor against me and do not want to forgive, I must remember that if they are a believer God has already forgiven him or her.

In Ephesians 1:7, Paul says, "In Him we have redemption through His blood." That redemption extends to the sins of other Christians against us. Then he adds, "The forgiveness of our trespasses, according to the riches of His grace." The forgiveness according to the riches of God's grace not only extends to our trespasses but those who trespass against us. In Hebrews 9:22, the author describes the impact of Christ's death in these words, "Without shedding of blood there is no forgiveness." The shedding of Jesus Christ's blood on that cursed cross providing forgiveness for all our sins, provided forgiveness for all those saints who have sinned against us.

In 1 John 1:7, the beloved disciple declares, "But if we walk in the light, as he is in the light, we have fellowship with one another, and the blood of Jesus Christ, his Son, cleanses us from all sin." The blood cleanses "us" from all our sins even against each other. Then he continues in 1 John 2:12, "I write to you, little children, because your sins are forgiven you for His Name's sake." The biblical expression "for His Name's sake" carries the idea of "all that He is and has done." The name of a person represented all of whom the person was and did. The sins believers have committed against us have been forgiven in His name and for Him.

Paul was the Lord's classic example in 1 Timothy 1:15-17. The Christians who had loved ones injured or killed because of Paul had to accept him into the church. They had to forgive his atrocities against them and the ones they loved the most. That must have been tough. As we can so clearly see, all of these passages include our forgiveness when we sin against others. We love to rejoice in this truth. Here is another equally important truth: these verses also include the forgiveness of others when they transgress us! In fact, here is a beautiful pattern: we are being forgiven for our sins against the brethren as they are being forgiven for their sins against us. There is forgiveness upon forgiveness. Often, we get stuck and do not want to forgive our brothers and sisters in Christ. Yet, we so desperately want God to forgive our sins against them. We cannot have it both ways. If we are to receive God's forgiveness, so are they! May this truth assist us in forgiving others.

An Ancient Portrait

Let's now take a look at the story of the Prodigal Son. This tale can also be viewed from the perspective of the older brother to gain some insight into why Christians do not forgive their brothers and sisters in the light of the last two principles mentioned. In Luke 15, the older brother was unwilling to forgive his younger brother after he repented. Let's pick up the story when the son returns and the banquet to celebrate began.

The son arrived at the house after a day's work in the field managing the estate. Suddenly, he heard music and dancing which meant people were celebrating something inside his home. There were no servants around. The outside of the estate was empty. All of them were serving the guests. He was standing there completely alone wondering what in the world was going on. He called over one of the boys who were playing outside, since the adults were celebrating, to find out what was happening.

He was the eldest son and should have been presiding over any celebration. Now, he had been reduced to someone asking children what was going on. They explained that his youngest brother had come back, and his father had killed a fattened calf. He may have thought to himself in disbelief, "What? That is impossible? That no good brother of mine is getting the greatest celebration any family can have? I have been faithful to my father all along and I have nothing!"

Then the boys explained further. His father had received his younger brother back safe and sound. The Greek words utilized actually emphasize the father's response to his son's return. The son had been received back in peace and with full restoration. This made the older brother very angry! So, the son absolutely refused to go into his own home! When dad found out, he came running out. What a great, warm, and loving father he was! He would not let the older son stay outside and wallow in his own anger, bitterness, and stubbornness. He pursued the older son in his sin as he did the younger in his. In his love, grace, and mercy, the father pleaded with the older son to come inside and celebrate the return of his dear younger brother. They were all a family again!

The older son could only think about himself. Instead, He rebuked his merciful father and described how he himself had served his father many years. He had never disobeyed him. The older son had never even been given a young goat, so he could celebrate with his own friends. This response is loaded with meaning. He turned this all around and made it all about him. Why was his father not concerned about his feelings? He had continually served and obeyed him. In his possessions and property, the older son had reduced his relationship with his father to nothing more than servitude and obedience.

He ignored the return of his younger brother and did not even appeal to the father's love for him. Why didn't he say, "Father, we love each other, why haven't you given me a celebration?" Why not even an appeal to love, however weak it would have been? Why? There was no relationship there in the first place. Notice, he tells his father that he has never even had a celebration with his friends, not his family. His buddies were all that mattered to him. He did not seem to care about his father or brother at all.

What a blow to the father! Neither of the two was worth anything to him. Then the older brother lets us in on a little secret. He was keeping tabs on his younger brother all along. He revealed the prostitution his little brother had indulged in and then asked his father why he would give his brother a celebration with a fattened calf. He threw his little brother's squandering of the father's goods into his face and still he was restored. The older son tried to rile his father up and turn his warm heart from compassion to bitterness. There was nothing but accusations.

Not once, did the older son ask how his younger brother was or even if he had repented. The father did not even explain himself. The father simply told him that he had always been with him, and all of his property was his. Then he explained that his little brother had been dead and was now alive; that is, his younger brother was dead to the family and was back. He was lost but now was found. The son was concentrating on the loss of their possessions and property, but his father was focusing on the restoration of their relationships and the rebuilding of their family.

Jesus told this story to point out that the Pharisees (older brother) had hard hearts toward God, our Father. They were concerned only about righteous works and outward religion, pomp, and circumstance. God is concerned about repentance and His gracious forgiveness. They did not truly have an inward, spiritual relationship with God but only an outward temporal relationship. For our purposes, let us focus on the older brother who was unwilling to forgive the younger one.

First, he was unwilling to forgive because he had never himself asked his father for forgiveness. Why? He thought he had never done anything wrong. He told the father he had never disobeyed him or ever failed to serve him. That is impossible. Since the older son had never gone to his father and begged for mercy, how could he in anyway understand how his father could show mercy to his brother? When we are not continually going before God with our sins begging for his mercy, then it is harder to show mercy to others.

How can we forgive when forgiven, if we think we do not need forgiveness? Those believers who think they are always right and have all of the answers have a tremendous difficulty forgiving the other person in a relationship. If this occurs, God will discipline that person to fully understand what a sinner he or she is.

Second, he would not recognize that his father who was the foremost person transgressed had already forgiven him. The primary person in that family was the father, if he could ultimately forgive then so could the other family members. The main person transgressed in a sin against us is God. If He can forgive them, so ought we. When a brother or sister transgresses us, we need to acknowledge that our Father has already forgiven that very transgression on the cross of Jesus Christ. We must view the situation from the perspective of God, not from our perspective. The older brother refused to view the situation from his father's perspective so he would not forgive him.

Third, the older son was looking only at what he had lost. He was focusing on the transgressions against him. As a result, he kept churning the sins over and over again. When his little brother had finally repented, he could not see past the sins. He could not comprehend what would possibly be gained. He could not see that he would gain his little brother back. Yet, this is exactly what the father saw. He looked past the physical and material to the relational. To find the right perspective, we must look beyond the temporal things to the deeper spiritual reality. Since the Lord God had forgiven them already, we must also forgive others.

26

A Modern Anecdote

One of my counselees grew up with a mother who had a serious alcohol problem. Since his father had passed away when he was about six, his mother did not take it very well. Alcohol was her drug of choice whenever, which was often, she felt overwhelmed by the kids (six of them), her job, the bills, and loneliness. Many times, after a drinking bout, his mother would arrive home and leave their front door wide open. When he awoke to use the restroom, he would see the front door open and think someone was breaking into the house. Other times, she would forget to buy food, and the kids would have to take whatever was in the house and turn it into school lunches. Sometimes, this meant a large piece of cheese or a small cereal box.

There were several incidences where his mother would fall and injure herself, and he would bandage her up. Then, he would fall asleep fearing she would bleed to death during the night. As he got older, the problem just worsened. Often, she would fall asleep on the couch with a lit cigarette in her hand. He would take turns with his other siblings to stay up late and watch her until she had fallen asleep drunk. Then, he would quietly take the cigarette and put it out to prevent the house from burning down. She spent much of the small amount of money they had on liquor and could not pay the bills. When bill collectors came around, they (the children present at the time) would hide behind the couch. This way the person would think no one was home. When he would talk to her about many of these events, she would respond with a long diatribe about the woes of a single parent who was doing the best that she possibly could. At nineteen, the mother finally entered a rehab program and sobered up.

After he had grown up and had his own family, he visited his mother on either Thanksgiving or Christmas every year.

Besides this time, he never called her or invited her to any of his children's events and activities. When his last child was close to graduating from college, she casually said to him, "How come you never invited me to any of my grandkid's functions when they were growing up?" This startled him. He could not respond because he did have an answer. For several months, he pondered that question, "Why hadn't he invited her to his children's activities?" He had spent every summer traveling to see his siblings but never his mother.

One day it dawned on him that he had completely walled her off from his heart. He had not invited her because there was no real relationship. He had no feelings for his mother. In fact, he was angry and bitter and had never forgiven her for what she had done. He had punished her unknowingly by not allowing her into his life or the lives of his children. Then, he decided that she deserved it, and that was that. A year later, the woman came to Christ. In the first year of her salvation, his sister gently confronted His mother concerning all of the problems that she had caused in their growing up years. She told her that she deeply regretted what happened and asked his sister for forgiveness. He decided if she called to reconcile, he would refuse to speak to her or even see her. The pain was too deep and the scares too numerous.

What could he do to break this anger and bitterness that had a death grip upon him before his mother called, so he could forgive her? I explained to him all that we have just studied in this chapter. First, he should compare the sins his mother had committed against him with the sins he had committed against God. God had forgiven Him and desired him to forgive His mother. Secondly, he must recognize that she had sinned against God first as she was sinning against him. God had already forgiven her for what she had done to him on the cross of His Beloved Son. He needed to ask the Holy Spirit to help him grasp these important truths so he could fully forgive her. After much prayer over several days, he was able to open his mind and heart to these truths and forgive her for the sins she had committed against him, as His Lord had already done on the cross.

A Personal Response

Dear Heavenly Father,

I have been harboring a grudge against a fellow brother (sister) in Christ. I have been so angry because (add name) sinned against me by (describe sin). Yet, I know that when your Son died on the cross, He died for that sin also. I realize that you have already forgiven the sin and expect me to do the same. Please give me the wisdom to know whether I should also set up a boundary or provide a consequence for this transgression to help (add name) learn not to continue this sin. I am very sorry for transgressing your righteous law. Help me to honor and glorify you in my relationship with (add name) and follow your Word. I pray this in the name of Jesus. Amen.

Chapter 3

Forgive the Lost

When people have transgressed us, sometimes it becomes difficult to forgive them. It may take some time. People can do some hurtful and destructive things to us, and we might get stuck in bitterness because we are unwilling to forgive. A way we can get "unstuck" is to consider all the sins we have committed against God. Once we realize that Jesus made no distinctions in forgiving us when we received His Son, it will be easier to make no distinctions ourselves. Why? God did not refuse to forgive us because of who we were or because of the gravity or extent of our sins. So, we are to do the same to others. If those who transgressed us are believers and we are struggling with forgiveness, here is another approach. We must consider this truth: whatever they may have done to us has already been forgiven on the cross. How can we not forgive what God has already forgiven? Regarding those who are unbelievers, we must view them much differently to get unstuck from bitterness. Rather than considering them as just wicked people who deserve punishment, we should see them as lost and desperately in need of salvation. This will be the topic of discussion in this chapter.

A Typical Scenario

Have you ever had or heard of someone looking out the window of his home and having the following conversation with his wife? He says, "Honey, you've got to come and see this! Do you remember that young guy down the street who we shared the gospel with the other day? The neighbor three doors down? The guy that told us he wasn't interested. He has two large garbage bags filled with glass bottles tied to his bike and ran into our car. The bags just broke right in front of our driveway. I can't believe this! Now, there's glass all over the street and a dent in the car. He's trying to pick up the pieces with his bare hands. Those pieces are way too small! Is he crazy? What a fool! Oh, he's going to pay, all right! There will be no forgiveness here! Honey!? What are you doing? Where are you going with that broom?"

This man had been caught in the act of being shamed by his forgiving wife. All he could think about was himself. His wife thought about the neighbor. The man saw his neighbor as a wicked man in need of judgment, and his wife saw him as lost in need of salvation. She ran out to demonstrate the love and compassion of Christ. The husband did not want to forgive him, but his gracious wife already had! This attitude sometimes takes ahold of us. Unbelievers hurt us in some way, and we do not want to forgive them. Then someone like this wife is able to. How does that happen? How could she show such forgiveness and we struggle with it? It simply has to do with perspective. She saw him as lost, not wicked.

A Scriptural Principle

Now we come to the next principle. The third principle is "we must view unbelievers as lost to forgive." This means we should view those who transgress us with the eyes and heart of God. In order to forgive unbelievers for hurting us, we must first see them differently. We must have the divine perspective of our Father in heaven. At this time in salvation history, God sees all unbelievers as lost and seeks to save them in His compassion. On the great Day of Judgment, the Lord God will see them as wicked and seek to punish them in His Holy Wrath. This is an such an important distinction that is well worth discussing.

A Biblical Explanation

We know people should be forgiven for everything they have done against us. The Lord Jesus makes no distinction in their beliefs or relationship to Him. In Matthew 6:12, during the Sermon on the Mount, Jesus declared that our prayers should end with "forgive us our debts, as we also forgive our debtors." In Mark 11:25, He told His disciples, "Whenever you stand praying, forgive, if you have anything against anyone." In Luke 11:4, the Lord stated clearly what the prayers of His people should entail, "Forgive us our sins, for we ourselves also forgive everyone who is indebted to us." There is no distinction between believers and unbelievers. Jesus uses the critical words "debtors," "anyone," "everyone." Forgiveness is extended to all.

This is sometimes easier said than done. Sometimes, we Christians may get stuck in bitterness and be unwilling to forgive. Perhaps, the hurt is so deep inside we cannot seem to get past the hurt. We may become terribly angry and wish harm upon those who hurt us, especially if they do not know the Lord. To overcome this difficulty, Christians must begin to think differently about those who do not know Jesus. When an unbeliever is viewed as a wicked, evil sinner, then it is easy to be bitter and angry. It is simple to curse them into the fire of hell without mercy. This is what happened with James and John, two of the twelve disciples of Jesus.

In Luke 9:51-56, the Lord was on His way to Jerusalem for the final Passover and His ultimate death. He sent some of His disciples into a Samaritan village to obtain lodging. The citizens of the city refused. They hated the Jews, and their feasts and Jesus was a Jew on His way to a feast. As far as they were concerned, this Rabbi was not staying the night in their town. When James and John heard of it, they asked the Lord if they could command fire from heaven to consume the town. The disciples were upset and desired judgment on these unrighteous people. Jesus rebuked them explaining that "He had not come to destroy men's lives, but to save them." When Christ came the first time to earth, He came to save the lost. The second time, He will arrive to judge the wicked. The first time, He views them as lost and desires to save them. The second time, He will have given them all the time they needed to repent, and they did not. Then, He will focus on them as wicked and desire to judge them.

In Luke 19:10, the Lord declared His desire, "For the Son of Man came to seek and to save that which was lost." Jesus spoke of unbelievers, especially Israel, as lost sheep, a lost coin, and a lost son. He viewed unbelievers as lost. We are to view them similarly. We might be in various relationships with unbelievers. At times, they may sin against us. When this happens, to help us in the forgiveness process, we must see them as lost. What does it mean to say the unsaved are lost? When someone is lost, they do not know where they are or where they are going. They cannot find their way. In many places in the New Testament, people are described by the inspired writers in their unbelieving state. For example, in Ephesians 2:1-4, Paul describes the unsaved as being dead in sin and sons of disobedience. He portrays them as living in the lusts of their flesh and walking according to the course of this world. He characterizes them as ruled by the prince of the power of the air and servants of Satan.

In Ephesians 4:17-19, he continues by describing these lost souls as being completely futile in their mind, darkened in their understanding, excluded from the life of God, ignorant, hard of heart, callous, and given over to sensuality and the practice of every kind of impurity with greediness. In 1 John 2:11, John paints a picture of the unsaved lost as walking in the darkness, not knowing where they are going because the darkness has blinded their eyes. They are stumbling around in the darkness of their own sin and wickedness and the lies and falsehoods of the Devil. When we are in relationships with unbelievers, we must understand that they are totally lost. They have no life in God (Romans 6:13), no Holy Spirit inside of them (1 Corinthians 6:19), and no Lord Jesus Christ to follow (Mark 9:41). These poor people have no spiritual power to change (Philippians 2:12-13), no desire to be holy or righteous (1 Peter 4:3) and have centered their lives on themselves (2 Timothy 3:2). The lost live by the impulses of their flesh. They don't get it, but we do! They are lost.

So, if we have a relationship with an unbeliever, why do we expect them to constantly behave like us? Why don't we anticipate them to act lost? Often times, our expectations are too high which makes us even more bitter and angry. You may say, "Aren't they also responsible for their actions?" Of course they are. If they do not come to Christ, they will be judged for every single unkind word or action they commit toward us. They desperately need Christ. Don't they? We could constantly condemn these people as truly wicked and wallow in our anger and bitterness. Or we can share Christ with them and continue in prayer for them. This does not excuse any of their actions toward us, nor the consequences for them. It does not mean they may treat us poorly. This simply has to do with our heart's forgiveness of them.

In Luke 23:34, the Lord Jesus was hanging on the cross, dripping with blood from the crown of thorns and the nails in his hands and feet. In His pain and humiliation, as He was slowly dying, He cried to His Father. For what? He asked Him to forgive His persecutors because they did not know what they were doing. He saw all of these people in the light of their lostness. They were dead, hard, calloused, and blind, but, most of all, ignorant. The Romans, who were doing the dirty work the Jews could not do, did not realize that they were crucifying the King of Kings. This crowd of Jews who were standing around the cross throwing insults and curses at Him did not understand this was their own Messiah. The frightened disciples, who had hidden from the mob, did not fully comprehend that as His death was at hand, so was His forgiveness of all on the cross. From His death would come the resurrection to a new life in Him. Even many of these rulers, who were caught up in their religious self-righteous pride, did not perceive that a new covenant in His blood had come. They did not see that a new and final priest was now making a final sacrifice for the sins of all men.

In the midst of this horrible chaos, Christ knowing all of this, looked down at their lostness and cried out for the Father's forgiveness. This obviously implies the Lord's own forgiveness in His humanity. Christians know through their understanding of the Scriptures that this prayer could only be fulfilled if all of these lost people received the soon to be risen Son of God as Savior and Lord. Yet, implied in the merciful cry to His Holy Father, is a God who became truly man, and as a man forgave His persecutors, tormentors, and scoffers. How could He do that? How could He keep from becoming bitter and angry, refusing to forgive? He saw them as lost!

In Acts 7:54-60, When Stephen preached before the Jewish council, he indicted them for their sin. They responded by rushing him, dragging him out of the city, and stoning him to death. He kneeled down, and cried loudly, "Lord, don't hold this sin against them!" Then he passed away. In his final words, Stephen took up Christ's compassionate mantle and begged his God for their forgiveness. Why? They were so utterly lost and blind. Once again, forgiveness from God must be obtained through and only through His Son. Once again, implicit in his words is his own forgiveness of these killers. Stephen was willing to forgive them because he saw them as lost. This sense of lostness brings deep compassion.

36

The Lord God has a heart for the unsaved and Christians are to possess the same heart and compassion for all those they know who are not believers.

In 2 Peter 3:9, the apostle wrote in light of those who were scoffing that Christ had not yet come, "The Lord is not slow concerning his promise, as some count slowness; but is patient with us, not wishing that any should perish, but that all should come to repentance." The apostle asserts that God is holding off His judgment day for the wicked in order to allow more lost people into His kingdom. Why does God do this? He has great mercy and compassion. This is God's time to pour forth His love, grace, and mercy. This is our time to pour forth our love, grace, and mercy. There will be a time for judgment upon the wicked (Hebrews 9:27), and in some way we will have a place as judges (1 Corinthians 6:1-4), but it is not now. This is the day of salvation, a time to forgive.

In Matthew 5:43-48, Jesus corrects the mistaken notion that one should love his neighbor but hate his enemy. The Jewish leaders taught that one should love his neighbor until he transgresses him, then he could hate him. Instead, our Lord commands us to love our enemies because we are sons of a Father who loves His enemies. We are to love, bless, pray, do good to, and meet the needs of those who hurt us. Why? God loves them and does the same. He causes the sun to rise and the rain to fall on the righteous and unrighteous. God looked down upon the world, saw so many lost people, felt compassion for them, and then sent His only Son to die for them (1 Peter 1:3). Remember, we were lost when Christ died for us! We needed someone to view us as lost, so we could hear the gospel message and receive Christ as Savior and Lord. Only then, could we find real forgiveness through Him. Can we even imagine if the person designated by the Lord to bring the gospel to us, looked at us, was appalled at our wickedness and sin, and then turned away?

An Ancient Portrait

This is what happened when Jonah viewed the people of Nineveh. In the book of Jonah, God had told him to go and preach to them; instead, he was repulsed and fled. He did not want them to be forgiven. They deserved judgment and he was going to make sure they got it. Why? These people were terribly wicked. Yet, the Lord saw them as lost and desired to give them grace. Then God commanded Jonah to travel to the city of Nineveh and preach against the city. So, Jonah boarded a ship at Joppa that was headed for Tarshish. This city was about as far away from Nineveh as one could get at the time. I am sure that Jonah had hoped God would give up on him since he was too far away.

While on his sea voyage, the Lord sent a great storm. This put the ship on the verge of breaking apart. The ship's crew started throwing the cargo overboard to lighten the ship's load. Then they cried out to their gods for help. While all this commotion was happening, where was the prophet? Jonah was asleep below in the cargo area. How could Jonah be fast asleep? Why wasn't he afraid? Most likely, the prophet knew God may punish him, and frankly he did not care. He would rather die than go to that evil city! Though he was calm in his resolve, the captain of the ship was not. The captain came down and screamed at him. He told him to wake up and call on his God to save them. He refused to do it. Then they cast lots to see which crew member or passenger had caused this storm? The lot fell on Jonah. They demanded him to explain who he was and what he had done. Can you imagine the tension in the crew as they stood there with this stranger that was causing all this havoc?

Jonah declared that he was a Hebrew who feared the God of heaven and earth. He immediately explained that he was a believer in the true God. Then he told them he was on the run from God because he didn't want to obey His command. They must have known right then that this man was special. He wasn't any ordinary Jew, and he wasn't disobeying any ordinary command. Something was seriously wrong. Then, they begged him to explain what the crew could do to calm the storm. I am sure they expected him to repent and offer something to "his god." This was a storm that was about to destroy them all. Even they knew this should be done. Jonah probably startled them by his calm and almost ridiculous response. He told them to throw him overboard. It was his fault, and he needed to go. Why didn't Jonah simply repent? God would have calmed the sea, and he could have shared the gospel with this amazing backdrop of God's power and grace.

The prophet could only think about those dirty, wicked, evil Ninevites. Nothing else mattered. The Ninevites were not going to be forgiven if he could help it, even if it cost him his life. Though unbelievers, the crew did not have the heart to follow his advice and throw him overboard. Instead, they tried furiously to row the boat to shore. This was a vain and useless attempt, but they could not kill him. The storm only got worse! So, they begged the Lord God not to hold what they were about to do against them and threw Jonah into the sea. Immediately the storm ceased. Now Jonah was flailing and thrashing about in his own stubbornness in the ocean all alone. The Lord could have left him there to die, but that has never been God's way.

He showed Jonah the forgiveness Jonah did not want the Ninevites to receive. God sent a great fish to swallow him. He was in the stomach of that fish for three days and three nights. While trapped there, Jonah began to reflect on what just happened. He remembered that he been in the depths of the ocean, the currents had engulfed him, and the waves of the ocean were passing over his body. At the same time, the weeds had wrapped around his head, and he had come to the edge of life and death. In that moment, he had felt far from the presence of the Lord. He knew he was exactly where he had desired to be. He was away from the Lord. Unfortunately, it was not what he had expected. It never is. As he was about to lose all consciousness, he turned back to his God and cried out in anguish with a desperate prayer for mercy.

He was literally lost in his own sin and stubbornness. Haven't we all been there before? He desperately needed some compassion from God, and Jonah was begging for His forgiveness. Though these Ninevites were lost also in their stubbornness and sin, Jonah hadn't thought that they might deserve either. Perhaps, the time had come to rethink this obvious contradiction. After having been swallowed up in the depths of the sea by a huge creature, he remained in its belly for three days and nights. It was here that Jonah began to ponder these amazing things. Then, he repented and thanked God for his gracious rescue.

When Jonah had finally submitted to the Lord God and decided to obey Him, God commanded the fish to vomit Jonah onto the shore. It was time to go to Nineveh. Again, the Lord issued His command to Jonah: preach to the city of Nineveh. These Ninevites were lost, and God wanted them found. So, Jonah arose and went to the city. Then, he walked from one end of it to the other proclaiming God's merciful message. He declared that they were to repent of their evil deeds or be destroyed in forty days.

This city was the capitol of Assyria which was the most powerful nation on earth. Who could overthrow them with such power? Humanly speaking, no individual or nation could, but Jonah was speaking for the Lord. His God can do anything that He desires. His God meant business. When the

King of Nineveh heard Jonah's message, he arose from his royal throne, threw off his royal robe, covered himself in sackcloth and ashes, and issued a proclamation in the land.

The king commanded that all people and animals put on sackcloth and ashes and fast out of sorrow and repentance for their wicked and violent ways. They should then pray that Jonah's God would have mercy on them and withdraw His burning anger and wrath of judgment upon them. The one hundred and twenty thousand people of the city obeyed from the greatest to the least with sincerity. So, God stopped the calamity that was about to come upon the Ninevites and showed them mercy.

Sometimes, like Jonah we view the unsaved as only evil and wicked. When they commit a transgression against us, we do not want to forgive them, nor do we desire them to come to Christ. Let them die in their sins! Our Father is not like this. He has tremendous compassion for them as He had for us. Must we forgive the evil, especially when it hurts us? How about when it hurt God's only righteous, beloved, holy Son? This is a total game changer in perspective toward all who are unbelievers. It changed Jonah's perspective, and now it must also change our perspective. God desires for us to see them as He sees them. The unsaved are lost and walk in darkness. All unbelievers do not spiritually know their right hand from their left. They should be forgiven.

A Modern Anecdote

Problems with fathers date back a long time. Every family has had one or more male family members who choose not to fulfill their responsibilities as fathers. They discovered it was quite easy to have children but extremely difficult to care for them. For the children, this often leads to issues in later life. One such child, now a man, came in for counseling. As he entered my counseling office, I was introduced to an upbeat, happy, and seemingly fulfilled man who didn't seem to have a care in the world. He was successful and happily married. His children were all grown up, educated, happily married, and successful also. He had become a believer in his twenties and desired to love the Lord with all his heart and obey him. His wife and children were believers, and his first grandson had just received the Lord Jesus Christ.

After our first session, I discovered that all was not what it seemed. He had glaring issues in his life which were under the surface, unseen by others, including his own family. He felt inadequate as a husband, uncomfortable as a father, and inferior as a man. He was so tired of these feelings but could not rid himself of them. No amount of prayer or bible study could solve this problem, and he did not know why. When feelings come up without present circumstances warranting them, then it's time to look into the past. During several sessions, we discovered that he had issues with his father.

His father was a heavy drinker and could be violent with anyone who disagreed with him when he was in this state. When the son was seven years old, his parents divorced over it. Then, his father moved out. As alcohol took over his father's life, he almost never visited his son. As a result, his son never learned the mechanical skills that he possessed, received any advice on the childhood or adolescent issues he faced, only saw his father shouting at his mother when they had to interact, and eventually forgot any relationship they had had before the divorce. In his son's mind, he was always a dark shadow which was lurking in the background never showing himself.

Sometime after the son had graduated from college, the father finally sobered up. The son thought perhaps now he would come around, but he did not. Suddenly he passed away. The anger and bitterness began to pour out of him like dark, murky water. He quickly became aware that he blamed his father for his feelings. His father had not been the example necessary for him to learn how to be a husband and always felt inadequate.

His father had not demonstrated how to be a parent to his children. As a result, he always felt like he could be a better father when he was actually a great "dad." His father had not taught him the mechanical skills that he so desperately needed to even fix the simplest of problems with his house or car. This made him feel like less of a man. He had not realized that every time one of these feelings occurred, he blamed his father. He felt like his father had robbed him of his needed preparation for manhood which led to his inability to experience the full joy of being with his family. This could not be recompensed. He could never have these precious years back.

I told him that he was completely justified in his feelings. It was the father's responsibility to fulfill his role in his son's preparation for his adult life, and his father had completely failed him. Now, he was gone and could never reconcile the relationship, but he still needed to forgive his father. Once this was done by faith, then the feelings would slowly fade away. When I discovered that his father was an unbeliever, I shared the principles in this chapter with him and we read the story of Jonah aloud. As we read that story, I could hear him quietly mumbling and muttering to himself. The Holy Spirit began opening his eyes to see that he was facing the same issues as Jonah. At the end, he announced, "I know what I have to do, please go with me." Several days later, we drove to his father's gravesite, and the man confronted his dead father and then forgave him. He had understood how lost his father truly was and how desperately he needed to be found.

A Personal Response

Dear Heavenly Father,

I have not fully understood how lost (add name) is. I now know that I am to forgive those who do not know you as much as those who do. Please help me to see (add name) as someone who is lost and desperately needs to be found, rather than as wicked who deserves eternal punishment. I ask You to soften my heart so I may forgive (add name) as You forgave me. Give me the wisdom to know whether I should provide a consequence or set up a boundary for this transgression to help (add name) learn not to continue this sin. I am very sorry for transgressing your righteous law. Help me to honor and glorify you in my relationship with (add name) and follow your Word. I pray this in the name of Jesus. Amen.

Chapter 4

Keep No Records

If we have a broken relationship with our spouse, partner, boyfriend, girlfriend, child, parent, friend, neighbor, fellow student, or co-worker, or even an acquaintance, we learned the Lord God desires that we go to him or her and reconcile the relationship through forgiveness. This includes what we do with past sins. The next step concerns any mental records we may want to keep.

A Typical Scenario

Have you ever had or heard a conversation with a spouse that went something like this? You say, "Wow! I have been waiting for this coffee all morning. (Sip coffee). Yuck! No cream. Honey! Did you remember to purchase the cream? (Person responds in the negative.) No! Why not? I gave you one thing to do and once again you forgot. This is the third time in a month you forgot the cream for my coffee. Last week, you forgot my shirts at the cleaners. The week before that, you also forgot to pick up the kids at school. I cannot depend on you for anything. (Talk to yourself.) The next time she needs me to do something, I'm going to forget! Let's see how she likes that! That'll teach her!" Notice, the spouse mentions the past mistakes over and over. Why do we keep bringing up the past? Why do we keep tabs on people who have hurt us? Why must we continue to punish our spouses, children, parents, friends, co-workers, or even neighbors who may have offended us again and again? It discourages them and makes us angry and bitter. This leads to the break-up of relationships, not the building up of them.

A Scriptural Principle

Once forgiveness comes, we must take the next important step. The fourth principle is "we must not keep records of the sins against us." Simply, we should forgive and forget. Obviously, we cannot actually forget, but we are to treat past offenses as if the transgressions are over, finished, and done with. When Paul describes Christian love in 1 Corinthians 13:5, he uses these very words to characterize it. He declares that love "takes no account of evil." This English phrase is two words in the Greek which mean "makes no record of it" or "no longer takes it into account." It was a banking term in the ancient world speaking of keeping a record of deposits and withdrawals in an account. It means keeping a record of someone's wrong.

Paul is indicating that love does not keep records. People do not demonstrate true love by keeping a record in their minds and memories of others' transgressions against them for the purpose of punishing them. Through forgiveness, the transgressions are forgotten and permanently removed from the ledger of our minds. This is a supernatural, divine act. Our memories of hurtful words or actions of a loved one may be triggered by a movie, book, song, or event, yet we make that memory of no account. It comes back up into the ledger of our minds, and through a conscious effort, we erase it once again. Every time it surfaces, we erase it. This is what God does for us.

A Biblical Explanation

This constant record keeping begins in the mind, not from the mouth. Our minds indulge in the continual rehearsing of what others have done to us, and this produces much anger and bitterness. These negative feelings bring forth strife and conflict as they transform themselves into harsh words and actions. Centuries ago, Solomon described this very process in Proverbs 30:33 when he penned, "For as the churning of milk produces butter, and the wringing of the nose produces blood; so, the forcing [churning] of wrath produces strife." A barrage of our transgressions is thrown at us or vice versa which destroys and demolishes our relationships. Why? This cannon fire leads to fighting, arguing, and quarreling which never builds and renews relationships, only crushes them.

In Proverbs 10:12, the king asserts, "Hatred stirs up strife, but love covers all wrongs." Real love does not write wrongs down upon the heart in order to use it against someone later; it covers over all of them. The recording of transgressions in our minds and repeating them in our words causes hatred of the offenders leading to disputes, clashes, and altercations. In Proverbs 17:9, he continues, "He who covers an offense promotes love; but he who repeats a matter separates best friends." Here Solomon is speaking of (covering over) not revealing the offense of one friend against another. This will promote love between them. When the offense is revealed, the one offended separates from the offender.

This could easily describe what happens in a relationship when people keep bringing up (revealing) the past offenses again and again, never "covering it over" in love. Suddenly, they will find themselves alone. In 1 Peter 4:8, the apostle reiterates this same important principle when he entreats his readers, "And above all things be earnest in your love among yourselves, for love covers a multitude of sins." Notice, Peter describes an effort that is earnest in our love for one another. This covering over in love requires an earnest effort to really love someone. It is so easy to keep bringing things up instead of holding our tongues. It is difficult and requires much effort to keep silent in love and forgiveness. This lack of record-keeping does not involve the consequences and necessary restitution one may require for the transgression. This does not in any way mean that the transgressor has a free ticket to do whatever they want and then say, "Sorry, you have to forgive and forget." This does not at all mean that we should never alter our behavior or set up boundaries in our relationships when sin continues to occur over and over.

Instead, this lack of record-keeping involves the response of forgiveness itself. Once our sins are forgiven, we should not have the transgressions brought up over and over again, so we have to relive them or experience the consequences again and again. When this occurs, it usually produces anger or grief that will lead to a real despair in the relationship. It will make us feel as if we will be held accountable for what we did the remainder of time we partake in the relationship. How can someone live in a relationship with another who says, "I may never get over this!" The reverse will also be true. We cannot put others through this torment and torture.

When Paul visited Corinth, someone had opposed him vehemently to his face. He had questioned Paul's motives and actions in ministry. After the church had disciplined this instigator, the man repented. Then Paul was very concerned about the man's restoration back into the fellowship. In 2 Corinthians 2:7, he admonished the church to "forgive him and comfort him, lest by any means such a one should be swallowed up with his excessive sorrow." The apostle was worried that after this one who opposed him had repented, the church would not fully accept him back. He did not want the church to shun him or avoid him. The saints were not to bring up his past actions against Paul because this would only lead to the man's excessive sorrow. If we keep bringing up an offense over and over, we are indicating to the other person that we have not fully forgiven him. This may lead to the transgressor being swallowed up in sorrow or despair.

This principle of forgiving and forgetting comes right out of the character of our merciful and compassionate God. Once people have received Jesus as their Lord and Savior, their sins are not only forgiven but forgotten. In Isaiah 43:25, God describes this process in the following words, "I, even I, am he who blots out your transgressions for my own sake; and I will not remember your sins." In Jeremiah 31:34, the Lord again proclaims, "And they shall teach no more every man his neighbor, and every man his brother, saying,' Know Yahweh; for they shall all know me, from their least to their greatest, says Yahweh: for I will forgive their iniquity, and their sin will I remember no more." In Hebrews 8:12, God announces, "For I will be merciful to their unrighteousness. I will remember their sins and lawless deeds no more." Now, it is not that the Lord does not actually remember; instead, He renders it of no account. It is over and done. It will never be brought up again.

In Isaiah 44:22, the Almighty God of Israel proclaims this, "I have blotted out, as a thick cloud, your transgressions, and, as a cloud, your sins. Return to me, for I have redeemed you." This passage describes the Lord's forgiveness utilizing a powerful analogy. He says that He puts a thick cloud over our sins so He cannot see them. All Christians must do the same when it comes to the sins of others against them. Is God going to bring up our past sins in heaven? When we die, will he bring up all our past sins and transgressions against Him over and over again into eternity? No!

Our sins have been nailed to the cross and remembered no more. Christ's judgment will be only for our reward. In 1 Corinthians 4:5, Paul describes it as a day of judgment which brings praise. The past sins were erased from God's ledger. Our evil deeds are gone. The wasteful deeds will fall away, and our righteous, holy deeds will be rewarded. So, when someone hurts us, we need to act like God does toward us.

We need to forgive them and forget the offense by rendering those offenses as of no account in our minds. They won't be brought up again.

An Ancient Portrait

The best example of someone who did not keep records is Jesus Christ Himself. When the Lord encountered Martha and Mary a second time on the way to raising their brother from the dead, He didn't bring up the past mistakes Martha had made. You may remember the first story of Martha and Mary in Luke 10:38-41. Mary was seated at the feet of Jesus listening to Him teach, while her sister Martha was in the kitchen making preparations. She became so overwhelmed that she stormed into the presence of Jesus and demanded that He command Mary to help her. Patiently, Jesus refused and explained to Martha that Mary had chosen the better part which was teaching over service. Mary was seen later at the house of Simon the leper anointing Jesus with oil in worship and adoration.

Their next recorded encounter together is found in John chapter eleven. It begins after the public ministry of Jesus had ended. Lazarus, Martha and Mary's brother, was very ill and deteriorating rapidly. The Lord received a message from Martha and Mary saying, "Lord, the one whom you love is sick." Jesus loved all three of them and they knew each other well. They believed He was the Savior. They knew He had healed so many people in Palestine, many of whom He did not even know. Now, their brother, someone He knew and loved, was extremely sick.

After receiving the message, Jesus casually remarked to His disciples that the sickness of His dear friend wasn't for the purpose of bringing on his death but for the purpose of demonstrating the glory of God. This was information only Jesus as God could know. He knew the world was about to see something so dramatic that people would speak of it for many years. To present His great glory to the world, Lazarus unfortunately would have to die for a short time, so Jesus stayed two more days. Though the Lord loved Martha and Mary, they would now have to endure one of man's most difficult experiences, the death of a family member.

By the time Jesus arrived, Lazarus had been in the tomb four days. A crowd of people had gathered around Martha and Mary attempting to console them. When Martha heard that Jesus had finally arrived, she came running, and she wasn't planning on their reunion being pleasant. Martha stood before the Lord and questioned Him as to why He did not arrive earlier and save her brother! She then implied that he could still raise Him from the dead if He so desired, since God always answered His prayers.

Before I mention what Jesus said to her, I want to take a moment to mention what He did not say. Jesus did not say, "Well, here we go again, Martha. The last time we saw each other you complained about Mary and her unwillingness to help you in the kitchen. This time, you are complaining that I did not come quick enough to save your brother. We are done. I have had enough! Let Lazarus rot in the grave for all I care."

Jesus did not respond in this way because the Lord was not keeping a record of all her wrongs. Instead, the Lord had forgiven her other transgression and was not going to bring it up again. This is critical to building strong relationships and is a good example of the principle we are studying. He did not allow what happened in the past to get in the way of the present. Instead, Jesus explained to Martha that Lazarus will rise again. Martha responded that she knew he would be resurrected on the last day and affirmed her faith in Him. He did not say he was going to raise her brother. After their time together, he asked for Mary.

I am sure that she left disappointed. She then went and sent Mary to Jesus secretly because Jesus wanted to see her. Perhaps, she thought Mary could talk some sense into Him, so He would raise their brother from the dead. They wanted him back! That is all they could think about. When Mary saw Jesus, she fell at His feet and questioned Him in the exact manner that Martha had done. Once again, if Jesus had come when they called, Lazarus would still be alive today. They had seen His power, they knew He could heal him, but He didn't. Notice, Jesus does not rebuke her for her temporal blindness (not seeing his death in the light of heaven).

Then, Jesus traveled with the sisters and the crowds of people to the cave where the brother had been buried. When he arrived, Jesus commanded them to move away the stone that was covering the entrance to the brother's tomb. Martha once again interjected. She commented that there would be a great stench because he had been in the tomb four days. This implied that the Lord Jesus simply wanted to see the body and perhaps say goodbye. Again, Jesus doesn't bring the record up and blast her for this third infraction. Instead, He simply reminded her that He said if she believed in Him, she would see His glory. Of course, she thought it would be on the last day not a few moments later. Since Lazarus had been in the grave for so long, all would know that what they saw was not a magician's trick. Jesus could raise even the dead!

When they removed the stone, Jesus thanked the Father and then commanded loudly, "Lazarus, come out!" Can you imagine the hush among the people? What? Did He just say what they thought He said? Just as suddenly, the dead man came hobbling out still being bound hand and foot by the wrappings that encompassed him. Jesus told them to free him, and let the man go. Nothing was said about Martha or Mary's indiscretion before the Lord. The Lord had forgiven them, and He did not keep records. Many believed in Him. So, when people sin against us, we are to forgive and not keep mental records of the offenses. This frees us from the torment of churning it over and over and keeps them from excessive sorrow or despair in the relationship. We are to forgive and forget.

A Modern Anecdote

A teenage daughter stomped angrily into my office with her mother in tow and demanded, "I want to go first." She explained that as far back as she could remember her mother took detailed mental notes on every "bad thing" (her words) she had done. If the daughter repeated even one of these, out of her mother's mouth would come a long list of infractions she had committed. It overwhelmed her and made her feel really stupid. She admitted that she was a bit clumsy and didn't always pay attention to what she was doing. I asked if she could give me several concrete examples. At seven, she was playing the game of Hide and Seek in the living room and knocked over a lamp which put a small chip at the base. She was reprimanded and spent the evening in her room. She told her mother how sorry she was. Then the daughter promised her mother that the next time she would be much more careful.

Two years later, the daughter was removing a box of her princess dolls out of the top of the closet, lost her balance, and the box came tumbling to the ground spilling out all the dolls. One of the dolls took flight and hit a figurine that her mother had purchased for her on a trip and broke its finger off. When her mother heard all the commotion, she stormed into the room, saw the broken figurine, and then screamed, "Okay, that's twice now. What is wrong with you?" After a detailed description of what she had done to the lamp, the mother marched her down the stairs and pointed to the chip. The young lady had felt so upset that she ran to her room, shut the door, and sobbed. The mother shouted through the door, "You are grounded for three days young lady! Once that figurine is repaired, it will be put away. That way you cannot destroy it."

At twelve, she made herself a snack and went to watch television in the family room. Her mom had told her many times to be careful with any food she brought in. The carpet was new. She decided to watch a scary movie and eat some nachos. In the movie, a monster jumped out from behind a corner and startled her to such an extent that she threw the plate up into the air. As the nachos, cheese, and salsa landed on the carpet, she gasped. She quickly ran to the linen closet, grabbed a towel, wet it, and began to wipe it up. The more she wiped, the worse the stains became. In desperation, she covered the stain with a small carpet she had in her room. She knew this was a dumb idea but could not come up with anything else.

When her mother arrived home, as always, she marched around the house checking to see if everything was in its place. The mother noticed the dishes in the sink, the towel with the nacho cheese, salsa, and bits of chip sticking out of the hamper in the hall, the small carpet on the family room floor, and her daughter nervously lying on the couch. She calmly walked over to the small carpet, lifted it, and gasped. The mother looked at her daughter sternly and whispered, "I told you to be careful. This house is full of your clumsiness." Then she rattled off a long list of the daughter's mistakes and sent her to her room. In response, the daughter sprang up and screamed, "This is all your fault. Everybody has to be perfect around here. I'm sick of it! I'm sorry, sorry, sorry! There! Does that make you happy?" As she left the room, her mother yelled, "I have standards!" From that time forward, it became one battle after another. When she was finished, she slumped in the chair sobbing, "I can't ever please you. I'm such a screw up."

This ended the session. In the next one, mom defended herself. After some time discussing the importance of not keeping records, the mother stared blankly at her daughter. Then with tears in her eyes, she responded, "That must have been horrible growing up and feeling like you can never please me. I love you! I am so proud of you and who you have become. I am really sorry for bringing up all those past mistakes." After this very moment, we began the restoration process. The mother had seen the importance of not keeping records.

A Personal Response

Dear Heavenly Father,

I am very sorry I have been keeping records on the many transgressions of (add name) against me. I am so thankful that you are not keeping any records on me but instead are forgiving and forgetting my sins against you. Please aid me in this same process with (add name). Help me to let go of (list the sins) he (she) has committed against me and truly forgive (add name). I want to honor and glorify You in my relationship with (add name) and follow your Word. I pray this in the name of Jesus. Amen.

DISPLAYING GOD'S GRACE TO OTHERS

Chapter 5

Restore Through Action

Once the transgressions are forgiven by both parties, it becomes time to begin the real restoration process to rebuild the relationship. Sometimes, it can be brought to the same level as it was before the incident. At other times, it returns to a lower level. Sometimes, it can actually be brought to a higher level of functioning with real effort on both sides. It depends on the effort of all involved as the Holy Spirit pours forth power into their lives.

A Typical Scenario

Have you ever had or heard a conversation with a spouse, sibling, or friend that went something like this? You say, "Hi! Well, today I finally worked things out with my mom. After all these years of struggle, I finally confronted her about all the things that she did in my childhood which were so hard on me. I was as gentle as possible without holding anything back. She apologized. Now I feel this huge burden lifted off of me, but I don't feel closer to her. I thought for sure things would feel different between us, but I still feel very little love for her when she is around."

If this were a scene from a movie, or a verse from a song, or chapter in a romance novel, then all the feelings would come flooding back. Then we would go off into the sunset and live happily ever after. This is pure fantasy and does not work that way in real human relationships. Neither is the opposite true. Once you have offended someone in a certain way, the feelings do not necessarily have to remain forever.

The person can get over what happened and the relationship can be restored. The past can be overcome. Getting "stuck in the past" may create a great dramatic moment in a movie, song, or story but never has to come true. Instead, any kind of relationship can be rebuilt if both parties desire it and will make the effort.

A Scriptural Principle

We now come to a critical and often left out step in this important process of forgiveness and reconciliation. The fifth principle is "we must restore the relationship through words and actions and allow the feelings to follow." In Galatians 6:1, Paul explains this important concept when he exhorts the saints in Galatia, "Brothers, even if a man is caught in some fault, you who are spiritual must restore such a one in a spirit of gentleness." These "brothers" Paul refers to could be sinning against us.

What do we do with these brothers who sin? "Restore" them. Here Paul is saying that as Christians, when we see someone caught in any sin, those who are spiritual should "restore" the person. The word translated "restore" not only encompasses restoration with God but all others who have been transgressed. In the apostle's context, the restorer is a Christian who sees a believer in sin. Yet, there are actually two other people who also might restore. These are the two people involved in a relationship that has gone awry: the one transgressed or the transgressor. This might occur after they have reconciled with the Lord God and now desire to reconcile with the other. In any of these three cases, there has been a transgression, and a restoration is warranted. This restoration must always begin with the Lord first. After this, the ones we have transgressed should then be addressed. This is God's divine way.

A Biblical Explanation

The next step in this forgiveness process is to restore. Sin destroys relationships and the Lord God desires for them to be restored. The Greek word translated "restore" means "to render fit, sound, or complete; to mend or repair what has been broken; to equip or prepare someone for something; to complete." In this context, it means to mend or repair what was broken. The word is used of a physically broken fishing net. In Mark 1:19 and Matthew 4:21, when Jesus called James and John into ministry with Him, they were in the process of "mending" their fishing nets. They were removing the holes in their net that would allow the fish to fall through. In 1 Corinthians 1:10 the Greek word is used of Christians being "complete" in the same mind and judgment. They are not to have any holes in their unity. The disagreement had to be mended, so all agreed.

In his first letter to the Thessalonians, Paul described his desire to return to them and complete what was lacking in their faith. He needed "to mend" their faith, until it was like a whole "net." In this way, their faith would be complete and mature (1 Thessalonians 3:10). When a relationship has been broken, it has to be mended. All the holes must be patched and repaired so the relationship is whole again. How does this happen? What do we actually do to mend or restore the relationship? Well, forgiveness is the first step which begins the mending process. Jesus gives us another key to the mending process in Revelation, when He demands that the Ephesians mend their broken relationship with Him. As the risen Lord explains to them how to accomplish this, we learn how we can do this very same thing in our relationships.

In the book of Revelation, Jesus directs the apostle John to send seven letters to seven different churches. In His letter to Ephesus, He begins with a description of their strengths as a church. In Revelation 2:1-3, Jesus comments, "I know your works, and your toil and perseverance, and that you can't tolerate evil men, and have tested those who call themselves apostles, and they are not, and found them false. You have perseverance and have endured for my name's sake and have not grown weary." Notice, the Lord Jesus began with a complement. He listed the things that He most appreciated about them and their relationship to Him.

To restore our relationships with others, we must begin with complements that describe the wonderful qualities that the person has and how much these contribute to our lives and relationships with them. This restoration process begins with the recognition that the ones we have transgressed or have transgressed us have made many contributions to our lives. I like to take some time to contemplate their qualities and contributions, before I start spouting off things that are of no consequence, insincere, or simply not true. This is not just "to butter them up" as one might say. These are true and sincere complements and reminders of their importance to us. This is step one.

Then the Lord Jesus mentions their exact transgressions. In Revelation 2:4, He admonishes, "But I have this against you, that you left your first love." The Lord obviously means Himself. Though they had endured persecution and stood against false teachers, they had stopped loving Him. They had gotten so caught up in the battle that they had forgotten who they were battling for.

We know the words we must use; now what actions does the Lord require of them to rebuild their relationship with Him? In the first part of Revelation 2:5, He describes their action, "Remember therefore from where you have fallen." The first action is inward. The Lord asked them to think back and to remember the time before they had fallen into their broken relationship. Why? They need to remind themselves of how good it was and how far they were from it. This is step two. We must remember from where we have fallen. I would think back to how great things were before the break down of the relationship.

Once this was accomplished, we would then compare the past with the present. It is not as good nor is it as fulfilling, because we have gotten so far away from each other. This is what is implied in the word, "fallen." When we have become upset, our flesh will plant thoughts in our minds like, "I never loved him," or "I never really had a relationship with her that was healthy," or "my parents and I really never got along." This body of death (the flesh) will drum up these sweeping statements and rewrite our history with the person to match our present feelings. This is not God's way. These thoughts only cause despair in the relationship and its quick destruction. This remembrance of the past relationship will provide hope for the future. It will also encourage us to put out the effort required to restore the relationship, so we can return to those wonderful former days. Once we had it "so good," we can have it again that way.

Our initial step, we have already discussed is found at the end of verse five, Jesus continues, "And repent and do the first works." Then the Lord Jesus asks them to repent. This we have already discussed. Suffice it to say, restitution and accepting the consequences should be inserted here as deeds of restoration. Then Christ commanded them to go and "do the first works or deeds" they had done from the beginning with Him. They must return to the beginning actions. It is these deeds that should take place again. The focus is not on the actions of love one does in the middle of a relationship, but the ones done at the beginning. This is a huge difference. This restoration requires the new, fresh, more intense deeds one does as a relationship is beginning to blossom. These are the actions that quickly build relationships. Therefore, step three is to do the beginning deeds. Notice, the Ephesians had to mend their relationship with their actions. He does not appeal to their feelings. Our mind decides what is right; then our actions follow. Once the actions have commenced, the feelings will follow them.

Now, what were these initial actions that the church did? They are the same actions and deeds every church did when it was established. In Acts 2:42, Luke describes them in these words, "They continued steadfastly in the apostles' teaching and fellowship, in the breaking of bread [communion], and prayer." They were praying (talking to God) and reading His Word (letting Him talk to them). The saints were receiving communion (remembering Jesus Christ's great sacrifice with thanksgiving) and fellowshipping with others (serving and supporting the saints in words and deeds). Apply this to our human relationships now. Our first deeds would be for us to talk with the people who need restoration and really listen to them. This is the word and prayer. We should look at their good qualities and the great relationship we had with them in the past and be grateful for them. This is like communion. Then, we should serve them and support them with words and deeds of kindness. Finally, we should be around people who would encourage our relationships. This is referred to as fellowship in the Body of Christ.

Whenever we take the time to have a conversation with, listen to, complement, show appreciation and gratitude, or serve those we have offended or have offended us, we mend a small hole in the relationship net. We must keep doing this until all the holes are mended, and the relationship is whole again. We should realize that this will take time to mend too. These nets were large and were spread out on the rocks and mended carefully. Why? They could not afford for the net to break again.

To restore a relationship properly means that we have to spread the net out and understand where the holes are. We must take our time to carefully mend them. The worse the transgression, the bigger the hole is. The bigger the hole is, the more time it may take to mend it. It does not matter what their response is when we begin the mending process, nor does it matter what our feelings are. We should keep doing the many beginning deeds of love and expect the previous feelings to return. Normally, this will be to their previous level. If we continue to do these deeds, then we may actually increase the feelings and bring them to a higher level.

If the feelings do not return and the deeds are being done, then it is time to pray for divine intervention on both our parts. The effort on both sides makes the difference. If we have an open heart and the willingness to put out the needed effort, the Spirit can do the rest. If we do this, we will have gained back our spouse, sibling, parent, neighbor, or co-worker. If they don't respond, we will have honored the Lord. In Matthew 18:15, Jesus declared, "If your brother sins against you, go, show him his fault between you and him alone. If he listens to you, you have gained back your brother." When we restore relationships, it allows us to gain back everything the other parties have contributed. This coincides with step two.

Another aspect of this restoration is found in Scripture's discussion of the "reconciliation" process. This word is found in Matthew 5:23-24, Jesus says, "If therefore you are offering your gift at the altar, and there remember that your brother has anything against you." We are on our way to church and suddenly we remember that another believer has something against us (whether we offended them, or they offended us), we must stop and then go and reconcile with them. Jesus continues at the end of the passage, "Leave your gift there before the altar, and go your way. First be reconciled to your brother, and then come and offer your gift." It indicates that we are to stop everything and "reconcile." The Greek word translated "reconciled" means "to make changes." This comes from a root word that is a banking term meaning to "render accounts the same." If there was any discrepancy between two ledgers, they would have to find the mistakes and fix them. Both ledgers had to be the same. We express this as "being on the same page." Just because someone will ask for forgiveness, doesn't mean that the cause of the argument or disagreement can be dropped. It must be fully reconciled. This is critical. Otherwise, the issue that caused the strife will never be fully resolved, and the strife is stirred up over and over.

The question then arises, who will start this restoration process? The answer is found in Galatians 6:1. Paul states, "Brothers, even if a man is caught in some fault, you who are spiritual must restore such a one in a spirit of gentleness; looking to yourself so that you also aren't tempted." When we transgress, we have to mend the relationship and bring it back to completeness. We must make the relationship full and strong again. Who begins the process? The first one who is spiritual! Paul says, "You who are spiritual." I always say, "First one filled with the Spirit has to take the first action to restore." The first one in the relationship who is filled with the fruits of the Spirit begins the restoration (Galatians 5:22-23). The Lord also expects the more mature Christian to take the lead if needed. If we have a broken relationship and we have been a believer longer, then we need to go.

This principle should also involve the many relationships we have with those who are unsaved. If we have a broken relationship with a non-believer, we are the spiritual ones and we need to take the first step. It does not matter who started it, or whose fault it is, once we are spiritual, we must seek to restore the relationship with all the parties involved.

Notice, it is to be done "in a spirit of gentleness." We should restore relationships in gentleness. We must not lord it over them because we are suddenly filled with the Spirit, more mature, or even are believers. Instead, we are to be gentle. Why? Paul asserts that we are simply a fellow, humble sinner before the Lord. Paul continues by saying, "looking to yourself, so you also aren't tempted." This means we could also be tempted to be bitter or not desire to make the first move. We could have just as easily been on the other side. Also, as we restore, we could fall back in the conflict again. The restoration could tempt us to be angry and bitter or get into argument again. So, we need to be careful.

An Ancient Portrait

In Genesis, Moses described a sibling relationship which had been broken for over twenty years. It had been between twin brothers who would not speak to each other because of one's deceit and the other's spite. Yet, twenty years later God would set up a series of circumstances that would force a reconciliation between these two brothers. These two were Jacob and Esau and the reconciliation occurs in Genesis 32-34. Though Jacob and Esau were twins, since Esau was born first, he stood to inherit two-thirds of all that His father Isaac owned. Yet, Esau cared little about it. One day Esau was famished, so his twin brother Jacob offered him a bowl of lentil soup in exchange for his inheritance. Foolishly, Esau agreed.

Later, Jacob impersonated his brother before an almost blind father by putting animal skins on his arms to also steal his blessing. This he did and left nothing but a curse for his older brother. Esau had had enough of it. He swore that he would kill Jacob as soon as his father had died. Once his mother, Rebekah, found out, she sent Jacob to her brother

Laban's family for protection. Then his twin brother Esau then left the household in disgust.

During the course of those twenty years, the both of them prospered financially and materially. They grew very large families and had households full of servants. Finally, it was time for Jacob to depart from his uncle's land and move back to his father's territory. To do this, he had to travel through Esau's land which was extensive. There was no way around it. He wanted to avoid a confrontation, but God's way has always been reconciliation and restoration, if at all possible. So, in God's providence, Jacob had to cross the land. Don't we do that? A holiday arrives, and we do everything we can in order to avoid a face-to-face meeting. We might even be in the same room but never speak to one another. The Lord God never acts this way towards us and does not expect us to act this way towards any others. Instead, He expects us to restore relationships through action.

So, Jacob took action. He set up camp near his property and devised plans for their reconciliation. Jacob selected gifts of his herds and flocks of animals for Esau: goats, sheep, camels, colts, cows, bulls, and donkeys. He divided them up into three groups according to their herds and flocks and sent a messenger ahead of them in each group. On three different occasions, Esau would be greeted with gifts of reconciliation. Each time, his brother Esau was addressed as "Lord Esau" and was told that Jacob was behind them hoping that these gifts would calm and satisfy him, so he would accept Jacob when they met face to face. After the third set of gifts, the time had arrived for the face-to-face meeting.

Jacob spent the last night before his encounter wrestling with an angel. Here God reiterated His covenant with Jacob and changed his name to Israel which would become the name of the nation in his loins. God assured Jacob that he did not have to worry about Esau because the Lord would protect him. The next day, Esau arrived. Jacob bowed to the ground seven times as he was approaching his twin brother. Here he was honoring him and demonstrating submission and sorrow over what he had done. This clearly indicated that Jacob desired reconciliation. Suddenly, Esau began to run toward Jacob. Would he kill him or embrace him? He grabbed him, hugged him, fell on his neck, and kissed him on the cheek. He saw the women and children who were with him and immediately inquired as to who they were. Then both his wives and their families bowed down. Esau asked why they had all come. Jacob replied that he wanted to find favor in Esau's sight and travel through his land on his way home. The implication was crystal clear he wanted to restore their relationship.

Esau then did something that could only have occurred through the providence of God. He declared that he did not need his gifts because God had provided for him. Then Jacob insisted that he keep them because he saw in Esau the face of God. God was at work because Esau had welcomed him favorably. Finally, his brother Esau accepted the gifts. Then, Esau suggested that they journey through his land together, and Esau would travel ahead of him. Jacob had to refuse because the herds and flocks had to travel at their own pace. Esau then suggested that he leave some of his men with him to assist in the journey. Again, Jacob refused. He did not feel the need, and so Esau departed. Then, Jacob followed at his own pace through Edom. The two brothers worked things out.

I do not think we see all of God's steps of reconciliation in this story because Jacob and Esau were never very close as brothers. Mom and dad had seen to that through their acts of favoritism. Also, they were extremely different people. The story does accent some of the most important points. Jacob did restore the relationship through his actions. There was gift giving and signs of respect. They stumbled over each other in their recognition of God's blessing upon each of them. Esau offered support for Jacob's journey through his land. They parted as reconciled brothers. This is all they desired. They both did what was right. They restored what they had through actions and allowed their feelings to follow. This is all God requires.

A Modern Anecdote

One day, a set of adult triplets (two men and a woman) walked into my office and described how distraught they were over the deteriorating relationships among themselves and their families. This occurred after their mother became completely incapacitated from a stroke. Since their father had passed away, they decided to allow their mother to stay in the family home with a live-in nurse. During this critical time, they each visited her separately or the two brothers would see her together but never the three of them. Then she passed away. When they met and began discussing funeral arrangements, it turned into an argument. This argument led to accusations concerning the future of their family home, furnishings, and savings. Once they reached an impasse, the sister went to complain to her pastor who referred them to me.

As the discussion began, it was not long before the two brothers were accusing the sister of trying to control and dominate them; in return, she was accusing them of ganging up against her. It was almost as if they were about twelve years old arguing over who would get the last piece of pie. It became very obvious that they had grown up in constant conflict. I asked them to describe their mother's interactions with them. They all agreed that their mother was a strong and domineering woman whose solution to every problem was simply shouting, "Stop fighting and go to your rooms." She never once took the time to discover what they may have been arguing about. This action led to a great amount of conflict occurring behind their mother's back. They began to learn very quickly to deal with things themselves which often led to many instances of physical confrontation. Since the sister always had her own room and she was a girl, the battle lines were easily drawn. The two boys constantly challenged the sister or vice versa. It would get so chaotic at times that things around the house would be broken. When their mother would demand an explanation, all three would stick together and claim that they had no idea what she was talking about.

This fighting and arguing continued until the sister got married and then moved out of the house. Then the mother would have monthly family dinners at her house, and she would accept no excuse for not attending. Either the three of them alone, with their spouses, or with their children would sit there as if everything were fine. When they left, the two brothers would not speak to their sister again until a holiday or these cold, bitter family dinners occurred. When their mother passed away, the pretense was over, the anger and bitterness poured forth, and the fighting once again began.

I explained to them that I could and would help facilitate the decisions that had to be made concerning the mother's funeral, but I would like to meet with them afterward. They had some serious relationship problems and needed to work these out for the sake of their children and their children's children. Often a dominant mother with children who have difficulty getting along will usually separate after her death. Thereafter, the aunts and uncles, nieces and nephews, and cousins will no longer interact with one another. Multiply that by several generations, and this family no longer exists. Though they were hesitant to act, everyone agreed when the children were mentioned. Once the funeral was over, they made an appointment to see me. It required some time to go through the reconciliation process, but it was well worth it. Once they had forgiven each other, we developed a strategy for them to restore their relationships through action. Then plans were created to strengthen all the various relationships among their families. Once these actions began, new feelings of love toward one another also began.

A Personal Response

Dear Heavenly Father,

I do desire to reconcile my relationship with (add name). Give me the wisdom to know what words and actions I can use to restore the relationship. Please provide me with the courage and strength to rebuild the relationship with those words and actions. Soften (add name)'s heart to receive my bold attempts to mend the net we have together. Help me to honor and glorify you in my relationship with (add name). I pray this in the name of Jesus. Amen.

Conclusion

As we conclude this book, I would like to leave us with some final thoughts about our God of forgiveness and what His Son did on the cross for us. First, if we understand the full extent of what was wrought for us on that cursed tree in order to forgive us, it will become so much easier to do the same thing for others. Second, if you read this entire book and realized that you do not understand salvation or have never received Christ as Lord and Savior, then I would like to provide that opportunity. Please do not skip this section; it may be the most important in your life.

From all outward appearances, humans seem "good" and attempt to live decent lives. This is man's concept of himself. This is not God's concept. The Almighty's view is that people all over the world and throughout the ages sin, sin, and sin again (Romans 3:23). This is a terrible and utterly destructive condition. Yet, they have ramifications that are far worse. These sins condemn us to everlasting divine retribution.

Though described briefly in the Old Testament, the Lord Jesus Christ clearly announced and proclaimed the future punishment to come. Contrary to popular belief, Jesus did not only speak of love, grace, and mercy, He also spoke of the coming judgment for sin. He declared that the judgment of sin would be everlasting punishment in a place He called "Hell." The Lord portrayed this place as an eternal inferno (Matthew 18:8) where there would be the weeping (from the sorrow) and gnashing of teeth (from the agony and anguish of suffering) continually into eternity (Matthew 8:12; 13:42, 50; 22:13; 24:51; 25:30; Luke 13:28).

Why must people face this horrific punishment? Though God is a God of love, grace, and mercy, He is also a God of great holiness, righteousness, and justice (Psalm 89:14,18). These attributes are just as much a part of His divine nature as His love, grace, and mercy. You have broken God's law as we all have, and the penalty must be paid. This began with the first man Adam (Genesis 3:1-7). When this occurred, His love, grace, and mercy surfaced, and a provision was made. Someone else would have to take man's place and pay the penalty. Someone who had never transgressed Him, who would never deserve punishment, and would fulfill all of God's Laws, would be substituted in man's place. This was the Son of God, Jesus Christ.

As the God-Man, He would pay the penalty for our sins in His death on the cross. Once done, the Lord God made only one provision for people to appropriate what His Son had done on the cross for them. This provision is receiving Jesus Christ as Savior and Lord. Though I cannot possibly share with you this good news in the confines of this book, I would love for you to consider purchasing my book entitled, *Finding The Light: The Kingdom of Heaven and How To Enter It.* It can be found for sale on Amazon.com. It is inexpensive and contains the full gospel message for your consideration. This message is so important and extensive that it cannot adequately be contained in a few pages at the end of a book.

If you are a believer, you must go out into the world and forgive as you are forgiven. These principles are to be lived and shared with others. You now have the tools to make your relationships last a lifetime. Go live them out and share them with others!

ABOUT THE AUTHOR

Dr. Donald Jones is currently a Christian Pastoral Counselor with thirty-eight years of experience in the fields of pastoral ministry, public education, and Christian counseling. He carries degrees and certificates from four major universities and from a variety of educational institutions. He has been a professor of Languages and Bible, a television commentator, and a featured speaker at a variety of events and seminars at churches, schools, and other organizations across the United States. He is a member in good standing of several secular and Christian professional organizations. Dr. Jones has been a published author since 1976. For further information view his website at www.donjonesphd.com.